1984

1984

BY GEORGE ORWELL

A NEW ADAPTATION CREATED BY ROBERT ICKE AND DUNCAN MACMILLAN

OBERON BOOKS
LONDON

WWW.OBERONBOOKS.COM

First published in 2013 by Oberon Books Ltd
521 Caledonian Road, London N7 9RH
Tel: +44 (0) 20 7607 3637 / Fax: +44 (0) 20 7607 3629
e-mail: info@oberonbooks.com
www.oberonbooks.com

Reprinted with revisions in 2014 (five times)

A catalogue record for this book is available from the British
Library.

PB ISBN: 978-1-78319-061-4
E ISBN: 978-1-78319-560-2

Cover design by john good
www.johngood.com

Printed, bound and converted
by CPI Group (UK) Ltd, Croydon, CR0 4YY.

Visit www.oberonbooks.com to read more about all our books and
to buy them. You will also find features, author interviews and news
of any author events, and you can sign up for e-newsletters so that
you're always first to hear about our new releases.

Acknowledgements

Plays are the work of many hands, and this text owes a debt of gratitude to the cast and creative team of the first production, as well as to the actors and academics who gave their time and ingenuity to development workshops, and to the brilliant teams at Headlong and at Nottingham Playhouse.

We would also like to especially thank for their invaluable input at all stages from inception to production, Rupert Goold, Giles Croft, and Jenny Worton; for their extensive support with the production, Henny Finch, Stephen Daly and Jasper Gilbert; for their feedback at various stages, Sarah Grochala, Daniel Raggett, Anthony Almeida, Robin Paxton, Jeremy Herrin and Bill Hamilton; for their time and patience, Rachel Taylor and Katie Mitchell; and for all their love and support, Zara Tempest-Walters and Effie Woods.

R.I. and D.M.

This adaptation was first produced as a co-production between Headlong and Nottingham Playhouse, where it had its first performance on Friday, 13 September 2013. Following a national tour, it then opened at the Almeida on Saturday, 8 February 2014. The original cast were:

Cast

WINSTON	Mark Arends
O'BRIEN	Tim Dutton
CHARRINGTON	Stephen Fewell
MARTIN	Christopher Patrick Nolan
SYME	Matthew Spencer
PARSONS	Gavin Spokes
MRS PARSONS	Mandi Symonds
JULIA	Hara Yannas

The production transferred to the Playhouse Theatre, West End, on 28 April 2014, with the following cast changes:

WINSTON	Sam Crane
PARSONS	Simon Coates

The production then went on tour and performed at the following venues:

Citizens Theatre, Glasgow (29 Aug–6 Sep 2014)
Theatre Royal, Plymouth (9–13 Sep 2014)
York Theatre Royal (16–20 Sep 2014)
Everyman Theatre, Cheltenham (23–27 Sep 2014)
Blackpool Grand Theatre (30 Sep–4 Oct 2014)
Nuffield, Southampton (7–11 Oct 2014)
Northcott Theatre, Exeter (14–18 Oct 2014)
Cambridge Arts Theatre (21–25 Oct 2014)

Creative Team

Adapted and Directed by	Robert Icke & Duncan Macmillan
Set and Costume Designer	Chloe Lamford
Lighting Designer	Natasha Chivers
Sound Designer	Tom Gibbons
Video Designer	Tim Reid
Associate Director	Daniel Raggett
Casting Director	Ginny Schiller CDG

Production Credits

Company Stage Manager	Simon Sinfield
Deputy Stage Manager	Amy Griffin
Assistant Stage Manager	John Fernandes
Trainee Director	Ross Levy
Animal Handler	EAB Animals

A note on the text

A forward slash (/) marks the point of interruption in overlapping dialogue.

A comma on a separate line (,) indicates a pause, a rest or a silence, the length of which should be determined by the context.

An ellipsis (…) indicates a trailing off.

The first production used multimedia and other scenic devices. The stage directions are presented here for ease of reading, not as a thorough account of the production decisions.

There was no interval.

FOREWORD: APPENDIX

The ending of George Orwell's final novel, *Nineteen Eighty-Four*, is notoriously bleak. 'If you want a picture of the future', Winston has been told, 'imagine a boot stamping on a human face – forever.' Sitting in a café, defeated, drunk and waiting for a bullet, he loves his oppressor. Winston loves Big Brother. As we all know, that's the end of the story.

Except it isn't.

After 'THE END', there is an Appendix, 'The Principles of Newspeak', that many of the novel's readers miss altogether. The American Book-of-the-Month Club, in discussions to publish the first US edition of the novel, demanded that Orwell cut the Appendix in its entirety (along with much of Goldstein's book) before publication. 'I can't possibly agree to [it]', Orwell wrote to his US agent in 1949. 'It would alter the whole colour of the book and leave out a good deal which is essential. It would also – though the judges, having read the parts that it is proposed to cut out, may not appreciate this – make the story unintelligible.' Orwell stood to lose at least £40,000 in American sales. To Orwell, clearly the Appendix was essential to understanding the story.

By the end of the novel, though, the reader should already know about the Appendix. At the first mention of Newspeak (on page four or five in most editions) is the only footnote in the entire novel:

> 1. Newspeak was the official language of Oceania.
> For an account of its structure and etymology see
> Appendix.

The reader might notice that Newspeak, oddly, is in the past tense. We might take up this invitation to read the Appendix before reading on. We might realise that fiction doesn't usually have footnotes or appendices.

The Appendix is fiction pretending to be fact. Written in a period long after the novel's 1984, a time in which the Party appears to have fallen, it re-considers the text that precedes it.

It is written in 'Oldspeak', our language, which should have been made obsolete, and concerns itself with the 'final, perfected version' of Newspeak 'as embodied in the Eleventh Edition of the [Newspeak] Dictionary.' In the novel's 1984, 'the tenth edition' is not due to appear for some months.

It refers to Shakespeare, Milton, Swift and Dickens and quotes the Declaration of Independence at length (the latter particularly unlikely to survive Party censorship). It finishes by telling us that '…the final adoption of Newspeak had been fixed for so late a date as 2050', reinforcing the point its own presence makes: that the final adoption of Newspeak never happened, and its 'principles' are so obsolete that they now need an explanatory Appendix. The final word of the Appendix (and of the novel) is '2050'.

O'Brien tells Winston Smith that he will be lifted 'clean out from the stream of history'. Yet, there he is, named once, off-hand, in the Appendix, telling us the name of the Records Department, 'in which Winston Smith worked'. We don't know how – but Winston Smith made it into history.

But if this Appendix is written by someone who has read the novel from the future and appended these historical comments on the language, what *is* the novel in their world? Is it a Party record on Winston which survived into this post-Party future? Something that didn't get into the shredder or the furnace before the records offices were stormed? Or is it something to do with Winston's diary? We don't know quite whether to trust it. The Party controlled all records. How has this 'account' of Winston's life survived?

According to the Orwell Estate, ours is the first attempt to dramatise the Appendix in any medium. It never felt less than 'essential': given the novel's interest in records and documents and their relationship to truth, the Appendix perfectly complicates the novel that precedes it. Treating Orwell's Appendix as 'essential' makes his novel something far more subjective and complex than simply a bleak futuristic dystopia: at the final moment, it daringly opens up the novel's form and reflects its central questions back to the reader. Can you trust evidence? How do you ever know what's really true? And when and where are you, the reader, right now?

R.I. and D.M. September 2050.

This text went to press before the production opened,
so may differ slightly from what was performed.

A clock strikes thirteen, a bell becoming digital.

A pin-spot on WINSTON'S face. WINSTON inhales, and looks toward us. He is a thin man in his late thirties.

An amplified voice is heard, though the speaker is unseen.

VOICE   In that moment, it became real: the thing
                  that he was about to do was to open a diary.
                  If detected it would be punished by death.

A desk lamp flickers on, its light unstable. WINSTON clutches a pen. A book is in front of him. He is alone in a wood-panelled room, shelves stacked with books, folders, archive boxes. It could be in a library, a records room, it could be in a school, a prison, a government building. Rooms like this have existed all over the world for years. A corridor can be seen beyond a long window. He looks around, anxiously.

                  There was no way of knowing whether you
                  were being watched at any given moment.
                  How often, or on what system, the Thought
                  Police watched any particular individual
                  was guesswork. It was even conceivable
                  that they watched everybody all the time.

A cream-coloured screen illuminates: a live-feed aerial shot of the blank page. The pen hovers over the paper.

In small, clumsy letters, WINSTON writes today's date (in the format 'April 4th'). WINSTON thinks. He scribbles out today's date.

In the centre, below the date, WINSTON writes in larger letters '1984'.

                  Winston faltered for a second. He did not
                  know with any certainty that this was 1984;
                  it was never possible nowadays to pin down
                  any date within a year or two.

WINSTON adds a question mark to the year.

                  Whether he went on with the diary or not
                  made no difference. The Thought Police
                  would get him just the same. He had
                  committed, would still have committed,
                  even if he had never set pen to paper, the

13

essential crime that contained all others in itself. Thoughtcrime.

The lights flicker.

Thoughtcrime could not be concealed for ever. Sooner or later they were bound to get you.

A deep red spot appears on the screen, expanding and brightening on the paper. WINSTON has a nosebleed.

Every record of everything you had ever done was wiped out, your previous existence was denied and then forgotten. You were deleted, annihilated: 'unpersoned' was the usual word.

WINSTON tends to his nose and the diary with a handkerchief.

For whom, it suddenly occurred to him to wonder, was he writing this diary? For the future. For the unborn.

The lights flicker – first the desk lamp, then in the corridor.

His mind hovered for a moment round the doubtful date on the page, and then fetched up with a bump against the Newspeak word doublethink.

WINSTON looks up.

There is a sudden, total blackout. We hear WINSTON'S breathing. Then, with a flicker, the lights judder back on.

A COMPANY of people are now present. The HOST, a man in his 60s, speaks, reading over WINSTON'S shoulder, a gentle, benevolent presence. It is his voice we've been listening to.

It seems to be the present day.

HOST   Doublethink.

How could you communicate with the future? It was of its nature impossible. Either the future would resemble the present, in which case it would not listen to him: or it would be different, and his words would be meaningless.

,

He was writing this diary for the future. For the unborn.

For us.

The HOST snaps the book shut.

This is the moment. A thought develops into action and everything, *everything* that follows becomes inevitable. Despite the consequences of doing so, as his pen touches the paper this man is attempting, to change the world.

There is a moment. The others in the room look at one another. WINSTON'S bemusement at his surroundings is mirrored by the others as they exchange glances.

This is a text which occupies a unique place in our collective subconscious – even if you've never read it. This account – its author – imagines a future – imagines us – and asks us to listen. But what is he saying?

FATHER   I had this feeling while I was reading it. I suddenly felt so happy to be reading!

General sounds of assent from the COMPANY. A CHILD has located a remote control and turns on a television.

MAN   I thought I knew it, but my memory was completely wrong. I had all these ideas before I started and now I'm – I mean – how do you begin to talk about one of the most significant things that has ever been put on paper?

HOST   Exactly.

MOTHER	It's wonderful. I really think it's wonderful. I really *felt* it. I mean, I'm not sure I always understood exactly what it's –
MAN	That's the point. It's about *uncertainty*, the impossibility of truly knowing / anything.
HOST	In fact, it requires us to believe two contradictory things simultaneously – and accept both of them. It's always about more than one thing.
FATHER	Austerity. / Unpopular politics, perpetual war, uncertainty.
MOTHER	Love. / The future. Hope. Humanity. Freedom.
MAN	Oppression. Torture. Uprisings. Revolution.
FATHER	Looking at the past and dreaming a better future.
MOTHER	Exactly.
MAN	But what it so beautifully demolishes is the whole notion of objective truth, of there being one set true reality. How do you know anything in this world is real?

O'BRIEN, spectacled, smart, formal, can be seen through the window, walking along the corridor. He is looking directly at WINSTON. As WINSTON turns his head to the window, O'BRIEN stops.

MARTIN speaks for the first time, looking at WINSTON.

MARTIN	Once you finish this book you become a different person. You don't feel the same. You don't *think* the same. It changes everything. And it will always be true. It's a vision of the future no matter when it's being read.
FATHER	It's a warning. It's a call to arms. He wants us to rebel. To switch off the screens and

take to the streets. To look at the world and say *this isn't good enough.* The way things are. The infringements on our liberty. The corruption. The lies. He wants us to do whatever it takes. Whatever / it takes.

WINSTON   Yes! / Yes!

MAN   Which is what I'm saying, or –

FATHER   Well, to quote the, er, at one point, it says 'we should never have trusted them. We should never have trusted them.'

MOTHER   It's all very…

Everyone turns to her.

Just…

We're inside his head. You know? He's imagining us and…

When you really think about it. It's all subjective.

She looks directly at WINSTON.

You are Winston.

,

WINSTON   I'm sorry?

WINSTON is troubled by a memory. A melody plays softly, 'Oranges and Lemons'.

The quality of the music changes to that of a mobile phone ringtone.

FATHER reaches into his pocket.

FATHER   So sorry, hang on –

HOST   Perhaps we might all –

FATHER   Sorry.

Everyone goes through their bags and pockets, searching for their phones, fussing with glasses etc. WINSTON has no phone.

For a moment, they are all absorbed by checking their phones. MAN laughs at his. The HOST moves to a light cord to try and turn on more lights: the bulbs burst. The MOTHER sings quietly under her breath, concentrating.

HOST   Is it –?

FATHER   Switched off.

They put their phones away.

MARTIN   You're seeing yourself in it because it's opaque. It's a mirror. Every age sees itself reflected.

HOST   Though he was shaped by what he lived through. These key figures, Chaucer, Shakespeare, Milton, Swift – all people the Party wanted to suppress! – they're each the product of a particular time.

MARTIN   If we were born in a different time, we'd be different people. Do different things. Think different thoughts.

FATHER   But nothing's changed.

MAN   Oppression. Torture. / Uprisings. Revolution.

FATHER   Austerity. Unpopular politics, / perpetual war, uncertainty.

MAN   Corruption. Deceit. Infringements on our liberty.

MARTIN   How can you say a book has changed the world when the world is still exactly the same?

MAN   Exactly. It tells you what's wrong, but it doesn't offer / an alternative

MARTIN   Full of fevered dreams and paranoid / hallucinations

HOST	Written by someone who knew he'd soon be dead.

A sudden screech of noise from the screen – feet stamping, a WOMAN'S VOICE yelling commands. It could be an exercise programme.

WOMAN'S VOICE	ONE, two, three, four! ONE, two, three…

MOTHER	Will you stop that?

The CHILD mutes the screen.

CHILD	Can I have some chocolate?

MOTHER	There isn't any chocolate. Just sit and read a book or something.

CHILD	A *book*?

MOTHER	Look. You know this already – in this room you don't exist.

The MOTHER produces chocolate.

FATHER looks at WINSTON.

FATHER	How about you? Where are *you*?

There is a subtle, sudden lighting change. O'BRIEN'S voice is amplified, though he is unseen.

O'BRIEN	I'm asking where you are. Right now.

A pause.

Where do you think you are?

The room returns to normal. WINSTON 'comes to'.

FATHER	Sorry – is there a problem?

WINSTON	No – I just – thought –

FATHER	I'm just asking where you are…?

On all this?

WINSTON	Oh, I –

MOTHER	Also, it does takes quite a while before it really…

FATHER   …gets going, yes, I agree. There's lots of
                  information but the action really begins
                  with the arrival of –

MARTIN   At this moment he was dragged out of his
                  reverie with a violent jerk.

MARTIN reads from the book.

*A WAITRESS walks along the corridor and enters the room. WINSTON
watches her, pouring coffee into people's cups, one by one.*

                  A girl had stopped walking between the
                  cubicles and was looking at him. It was a
                  girl with dark hair whom he often passed
                  in the corridors. He did not know her
                  name, but he knew that she worked in
                  the Fiction Department. A narrow scarlet
                  sash, emblem of the Anti-Sex League, was
                  wound several times round her waist. It was
                  always the women and above all the young
                  ones, who were the most bigoted adherents
                  of the Party, the swallowers of slogans and
                  the amateur spies. But this particular girl
                  gave him the impression of being more
                  dangerous than most. The idea crossed
                  his mind that she might be an agent of the
                  Thought Police.

                  And now she was looking at him.

                  A horrible pang of terror went through
                  him.

                  Why was she watching him?

*The WAITRESS starts pouring coffee into the cup in front of WINSTON.
He looks at her. The melody plays.*

WAITRESS   Real coffee.

                  Is it late or is it early? The clock must have
                  stopped.

There is a buzzing sound and the lights flicker.

WINSTON   What did you say?

Suddenly she stops pouring and WINSTON 'comes to'.

Shakespeare.

FATHER fumbles with his phone, which is where the melody is coming from.

FATHER   So sorry, hang on –

HOST   Perhaps we might all –

FATHER   Sorry.

Everyone else turns the phones off, fussing with phones, glasses. The HOST moves to a light cord to try and turn on some more lights: the bulbs burst. WINSTON blinks at the repeat and mouths along with MARTIN.

HOST   Is it – ?

FATHER   Switched off.

MARTIN   You're seeing yourself in it because it's opaque. It's a mirror. Every age sees itself reflected.

WINSTON stands.

WINSTON   What?

The lights flicker, then cut out completely, plunging the room into darkness.

MOTHER   What's happening?

FATHER   Power.

MAN   Gone.

HOST   Sorry everyone, remain still, stay in your seats, this has happened before, remain still, let me just see if I can…

The lights come up. WINSTON is in the same place but everyone else has vanished. He looks around, panicked.

WINSTON shuts his eyes tight. Opens them again. Nothing has changed.

O'BRIEN'S voice is amplified.

O'BRIEN   Winston. Winston Smith. Where do you
            think you are?

WINSTON   Who is this?

O'BRIEN   Now, Winston, you know that already. You
            have always known it.

WINSTON   This is all wrong this is all wrong this is all
            wrong.

O'BRIEN   We shall meet, Winston, in the place where
            there is no darkness.

The CHILD has appeared in the room. She blows a whistle loudly.

CHILD   THOUGHT CRIMINAL! REMAIN
            STILL! You're a traitor! You're a thought
            criminal!

            Aren't you?
            You know you are.
            I know you are.
            She knows.

JULIA walks through the corridor.

            SHE. KNOWS.

*There's an urgent knock on the door. WINSTON is sure it's JULIA and
panics. He turns off the desk lamp above the diary. But then:*

*MRS PARSONS (MOTHER) bursts into the room. She is frightened of her
daughter and wears a fixed smile. She's slow and her CHILD is fast.*

MRS PARSONS   *(To CHILD.)* Can you please stay in the flat, I
              don't know how many times I have to.

              (To WINSTON.) I'm so sorry.

WINSTON is looking at her.

WINSTON   Do you know me?

MRS PARSONS	You are Winston. You work with my husband? We live next door. It's just me – Comrade Parsons? Are you alright?
WINSTON	Do I – ? How long have I lived here?
MRS PARSONS	You've always lived here.
CHILD	Can I have some chocolate?
MRS PARSONS	There isn't any chocolate. You know this already – sorry – can you *please* just –
	(To WINSTON.) I just wanted to see if you'd had trouble with the power as well. If it's just me or if they're expecting some airstrikes or…
WINSTON	I don't know what's happening.
MRS PARSONS	No. Right. Oh well.
CHILD	THOUGHT CRIMINAL!

They freeze and look at the CHILD. MRS PARSONS smiles nervously.

MRS PARSONS	She's a bit enthusiastic, I'm afraid! Hasn't been out today. Youth League tomorrow – gives them a chance to –
CHILD	I want to watch the executions.
MRS PARSONS	Okay I'm just –
CHILD	NOW.

The CHILD looks at WINSTON.

Big Brother is watching you.

A bomb drops nearby. WINSTON jumps. MRS PARSONS shuts the door behind her. WINSTON is alone. The desk lamp comes on, illuminating the diary. WINSTON turns past the title page and reveals handwritten pages, full of text:

DOWN WITH BIG BROTHER

DOWN WITH BIG BROTHER

DOWN WITH BIG BROTHER

He's astonished. He slams it shut, picks it up, terrified.

The HOST has become CHARRINGTON. He pulls the cord, just as before: this time, the lights illuminate.

CHARRINGTON   You've got a good eye.

The diary. Well, keepsake album. Beautiful bit of paper, that is. Cream-laid, it used to be called. There's been no paper like that made for…oh, I dare say fifty years.

You're not the first Party Member in here. Last lot took the glassware. And the metal pieces. To melt them down, you understand.

But you're different. I knew that straight away. I'll sell it to you.

CHARRINGTON points to the diary.

WINSTON   I've no need for a –

CHARRINGTON   Not my business what you need it for.

WINSTON   Where am I?

CHARRINGTON   The one place in the world where the past still exists. My shop. Antiques. As was, anyway: who cares about old things any more?

CHARRINGTON produces a snowglobe.

Now. This is what you want.

Thick glass. That wasn't made less than a hundred years ago. More, by the look of it. They never found it when they were in here. There's another room in the back. Not even a telescreen in there: never bothered.

WINSTON   No telescreen?

24

CHARRINGTON   It's just for storage, now, after all. There's a
               little yard too. It's ragged, but it's discreet.
               Used to be our garden. We lived in that
               room, my wife and – until she –

               ,

He shakes the snowglobe. It fills with snow.

WINSTON   It's a beautiful thing.

CHARRINGTON   It is a beautiful thing. But there's not many
               that'd say so these days. That building
               inside's a ruin now. Bombed years ago. It was
               a church at one time, St Clement's Danes,
               its name was. "Oranges and lemons', say the
               bells of St Clement's.'

WINSTON   What's that?

CHARRINGTON   Oh. "Oranges and lemons', say the bells of St
               Clement's.' That was a rhyme we had when
               I was a little boy. How it goes on I don't
               remember. Went out of my head. Long gone.

               'Oranges and lemons', say the bells of St Clement's,
               'You owe me three farthings', say the bells of St Martin's…

               Feels to me like it belongs to you.

WINSTON   The / diary.

CHARRINGTON   Keepsake album.

               ,

WINSTON   Yes.

CHARRINGTON   If you're interested in anything else, we could
               wrap them together. I don't mean these bits.
               There's a few more pieces in the other room.
               Things I forgot to mention to the officials.

               If you want a glance in there, you'll do with a
               light.

Through there. Along the corridor. It's the only door.

CHARRINGTON gestures to the cupboard. WINSTON opens the door – and it contains mops and a few old clothes. We can see right to the back.

,

WINSTON feels faint. The sound of blood rushing to his head, everything submerged.

WINSTON   Oranges and lemons…

As WINSTON starts to collapse, the room is plunged into darkness. Then torches illuminate.

MAN   If he's been electrocuted.

MOTHER   He hasn't.

MAN   If he's been electrocuted we shouldn't touch him.

MOTHER   Lift him.

They lift WINSTON into his chair.

HOST   He's coming. Now. With water. Are you feeling alright?

MOTHER   The power's gone out, don't worry. We're still here. I think you might have fainted, or –

HOST   Do you know where you are? Just get your breath back. Take your time.

The FATHER waves his fingers in front of WINSTON'S face.

FATHER   How many fingers? How many fingers?

HOST   When you're ready, we're going to have to evacuate.

FATHER   Did you see the café outside / when you came in?

HOST   Everything's going to be fine. Everything's going to be fine.

The lights flicker – JULIA is visible in the corridor - and then blackout.
The torches go out. From the screen, a klaxon sounds.

TELESCREEN   Attention comrades! The Ministry of Peace
                  has learnt that the Brotherhood is plotting
                  a major attack. Big Brother has raised us to
                  high alert. Remain vigilant. Brotherhood
                  members or Emmanuel Goldstein himself
                  could be undercover in your building.

                  Big Brother is watching you.

Another klaxon. Another voice takes over.

WOMAN'S VOICE   And resuming! Standing up straight! Arms
                  bending and stretching! Take your time by
                  me. ONE, two three, four! ONE, two…

                  Smith!

                  6079 Smith W.!

WINSTON looks up at the screen.

                  Yes, YOU! With your head on the table!

                  Stand when I'm speaking to you!

WINSTON stands, he has not yet recovered.

                  Look at yourself. Where do you think you
                  are? Stand up straight.

He does.

                  Now touch your toes.

He tries.

                  You're not trying. Lower please!

                  BEND!

He is struggling.

                  Short breaths out, please! BEND, two
                  three, four! BEND, two three four!

WINSTON touches his toes.

That's better comrade! We can't all be
fighting on the Eurasian front but at least
we can all keep FIT.

SYME (MAN) walks over to WINSTON and hands him a glass of water.
He's holding a canteen tray with a plate of food and cutlery on it.
They are in the work canteen.

MARTIN   Victory gin!

SYME   You don't really appreciate Newspeak,
                  Winston. Do you? Not really.

SYME speaks with his mouth full.

You don't have to be an expert to know that
Newspeak is the only language in the world
whose vocabulary gets smaller every year.

It's a beautiful thing, the destruction of
words. Of course the great wastage is in
the verbs and adjectives, but there are
hundreds of nouns that can be got rid of
as well. It isn't only the synonyms; there
are also the antonyms. After all, what
justification is there for a word which is
simply the opposite of some other word?
A word contains its opposite in itself. Take
'good', for instance. If you have a word like
'good', what need is there for a word like
'bad'? 'Ungood' will do just as well – better,
because it's an exact opposite, which the
other is not. Don't you see the beauty of
that, Winston? It was Big Brother's idea
originally, of course.

In the end we shall make thoughtcrime
literally impossible, because there will be
no words in which to express it. Even now,
of course, there's no reason or excuse for
committing thoughtcrime. It's merely a
question of self-discipline, realitycontrol.
But in the end there won't be any need

even for that. The Project will be complete
when the language is perfect.

Has it ever occurred to you, Winston, that
by the year 2050, at the very latest, not a
single human being will be alive who could
understand such a conversation as we are
having now?

WINSTON	Except –
SYME	By 2050 – earlier, probably – all real knowledge of Oldspeak will have disappeared. The whole *climate* of thought will be different. In fact there will be no thought, as we understand it now. Orthodoxy means not thinking – not needing to think. Orthodoxy is unconsciousness.

Here's Parsons.

PARSONS (FATHER) wears shorts.

PARSONS	Syme. Smith. Smith, Syme!
SYME	Parsons.
PARSONS	Just got back from the Community Centre. So refreshing.

PARSONS sits down with them. SYME doesn't like him.

You know what that girl of mine did last
Saturday? Absolutely brilliant. Pleased
as punch. Her troop are on a hike out
Berkhamsted way. Two of her friends go
with her and they all slip off – following this
man. They keep on his tail for two hours,
right through the woods, right through
the countryside, and when they get into
Amersham they hand him right over to the
officials.

,

29

WINSTON	Why did – ?
PARSONS	My kid made sure he was some kind of enemy agent. Might have been parachuted in or something. But this is the bit that's really brilliant. What put her onto him in the first place?

,

SYME	Shoes.
PARSONS	He was wearing a funny pair of shoes!
SYME	He told me before.
PARSONS	So chances are he was a foreigner. Pretty smart, right? Pretty smart for a seven year old.

JULIA (WAITRESS) walks along the corridor as before. WINSTON watches her as she enters the room. He is terrified of her and is only half-listening to PARSONS.

WINSTON	What happened to the man?
PARSONS	Couldn't say. But wouldn't be surprised if it's –

PARSONS aims an imaginary rifle and pulls the trigger. There is a loud gunshot which only WINSTON hears.

SYME	Good.
PARSONS	I mean, there is a war on.

JULIA comes closer, sits at the other end of the table. WINSTON takes a knife from the table and holds it.

Did I ever tell you about the time my daughter set fire to that old woman's skirt because her and her friends – well, they saw her leaning against a poster of Big Brother! Burned her quite badly. Little beggars! But it's amazing how much they pick up on – how much they notice –

It's a first-rate training training training they give them in the Spies nowadays – better than in my day, even. You know what they've served them all out with now? Devices for listening through keyholes! My little girl brought one home the other night – tried it out on our bedroom door, and reckoned she could hear twice as much as with her ear to the hole. Of course it's only a toy, mind you. Still, gives 'em the right idea, eh? She's thoughtpolice in the making.

JULIA stands. WINSTON tenses.

Get right inside your head. Absolutely brilliant.

JULIA exits. WINSTON is relieved.

The TELESCREEN speaks. Everyone on stage falls silent to listen to it.

TELESCREEN   Comrades! Attention, comrades! We have glorious news for you. The armies of Oceania and our Eastasian allies have won a decisive victory against our enemies in Eurasia. Big Brother has decided to celebrate by raising the chocolate ration to twenty grams.

SYME   Well, you can't complain when you're given more chocolate.

PARSONS   It's absolutely *brilliant.*

WINSTON hears O'BRIEN'S voice.

O'BRIEN   Winston. Where do you think you are?

WINSTON   The chocolate…

O'BRIEN   Think, Winston.

WINSTON   I'm at work. In the canteen.

O'BRIEN   Good. And?

The canteen fades away.

WINSTON   And the Party is saying that the chocolate ration has been raised to twenty grams. But I think I remember... I'm sure I remember...

O'BRIEN   Yes.

WINSTON   Yesterday they raised it to twenty grams. Every day the chocolate ration increases to twenty grams. It's *always* twenty grams. And everyone pretends they don't see it. Or perhaps they really can't.

The desk lamp comes on. WINSTON opens the diary to a random page. The pages are filled with writing.

O'BRIEN   Doublethink.

WINSTON   Is this how it feels to go mad? Am I imagining your voice?

       No. You can hear me.

O'BRIEN is in the corridor. We, for the first time, associate O'BRIEN'S face with his voice.

O'BRIEN   I can hear you, Winston.

WINSTON switches on the desklamp.

It flickers. He opens the book.

WINSTON   I'm writing a diary. An account. *Evidence* – that in all this insanity there was one person who held tight to the truth. I can see what the future will look like. A future free of the Party. People free to talk and think. All this will change. It has to change.

WINSTON roars with the effort of thinking for himself.

       I'm not mad. There *is* truth and there are facts. Freedom is the freedom to say that two plus two make four. Because *it does.*

Two plus two make four. Two plus two make four.

A page of endless "2+2=4".

I thought I was writing for the future, the unborn. But now I think I'm writing for you.

O'BRIEN We shall meet, Winston…

WINSTON/O'BRIEN …in the place where there is no darkness.

An abrupt lighting change.

SPEAKWRITE Name.

,

Name.

WINSTON …Winston Smith.

SPEAKWRITE Confirmed. Ministry of Truth. Welcome Comrade 6079, Winston Smith.

A beep.

Project active. Please rectify all references to unperson 5988, name Ogilvy. Rewrite fullwise.

WINSTON Call. Birth records. Search. Comrade Ogilvy.

A name in a handwritten register of births, marriages and deaths.

Select Ogilvy informationplus. Unwrite.

The name is selected.

SPEAKWRITE Assent unwrite?

WINSTON Assent.

The line vanishes from view. The other two lines are rapidly repixellated to join in the middle.

WINSTON Call. Newspapers. Search. Ogilvy.

SPEAKWRITE   Two records.

An article this time. We zoom in on a paragraph, reading 'also commended by Big Brother for their bravery and diligence in the face of hardship and challenge were Comrades Jones, O'Flynn, Petrie and Ogilvy. Hardship conditions had meant that…'

WINSTON   Select Ogilvy. Unwrite.

The name is selected.

SPEAKWRITE   Assent unwrite?

WINSTON   Assent.

The line vanishes from view, and the sentence is corrected '…and Petrie'. A newspaper article about Ogilvy. Ogilvy beams into the camera, in a café. We zoom to see Ogilvy's face and the caption underneath it reads 'Pictured: Comrade Ogilvy…'

    Article. Totalunwrite.

SPEAKWRITE   Assent totalunwrite?

WINSTON   Assent.

A white screen.

    Call file. Comrade Ogilvy. Unwrite.

SPEAKWRITE   Comrade Ogilvy. Forty-eight records.

A montage of images, an entire life, beginning with a baby photograph, moving through Ogilvy as a toddler, a young boy standing with a young girl, a young man at work and with his family, and moving through to Ogilvy as a man in his forties.

    Assent unwrite?

WINSTON   Assent.

    Call. All files. Search. All records. Comrade Ogilvy. 5988.

SPEAKWRITE   No records. Number is unallocated. Person does not exist.

A klaxon sounds. The telescreen flickers into life.

TELESCREEN   Attention comrades. The Two Minutes Hate will begin in ten seconds.

The lights dim. A countdown. Everyone arranges themselves to see the screen. O'BRIEN enters the stage for the first time – WINSTON is very aware of him. JULIA also enters. They sit on either side of him. WINSTON is surrounded.

The countdown reaches zero. A moment of silence as all the lights black out.

Then: a horrifically loud screaming, grinding, metallic, noise. The characters look out to the audience – we see the screen.

The sound stops abruptly.

         Another enemy of the Party has been captured. A member of the Brotherhood has confessed to conspiring to kill Big Brother and to attack our freedom.

A head-and-shoulders shot of a THOUGHTCRIMINAL, a bag over his head. The bag is taken off. He squints into the light.

'

THOUGHTCRIMINAL I am a thoughtcriminal.

JULIA   *(Looking at WINSTON.)* Thoughtcriminal.

THOUGHTCRIMINAL I have committed crimes against the Party. I am guilty of conspiracy to destroy, to inflict violence, to create chaos, to bring about the deaths of countless innocent people. I was brainwashed by the teachings of the traitor Emmanuel Goldstein.

         I was initiated into the Brotherhood. But I see now that Goldstein is the enemy. He hates freedom. He hates our way of life. I repent. I reject Goldstein's lies.

Footage of GOLDSTEIN speaking straight to camera. Everyone shouts, drowning out GOLDSTEIN. The crowd roar and scream at the screen with increasing volume and ferocity.

GOLDSTEIN   Oceania must wake up. This is the first period in all of human history where the future has *less* to offer us than the present, and the present less than the past. It cannot be allowed to continue. We need to stop *dreaming*. We need to wake up. We need to *act*. We need to know the truth.

GOLDSTEIN'S face morphs into that of a sheep. The crowd bleat in unison.

We must fight for our freedom. Freedom of speech. Freedom of language. Down with Newspeak. Freedom of the Press. Freedom of Assembly. Freedom of thought.

Suddenly, everything submerges – WINSTON is amplified amid the din.

WINSTON   I'm not alone. The Brotherhood exists. Resistance exists. I have to do something. Whatever the consequences. I have to do something. Down with the Party! Down with Big Brother!

They'll shoot me I don't care they'll shoot me in the back of the head *I don't care* down with Big Brother they always shoot you in the back of the head I don't care down with Big Brother.

DOWN WITH BIG BROTHER! DOWN WITH BIG BROTHER! DOWN WITH BIG BROTHER! DOWN WITH BIG BROTHER!

The Hate returns to normal, everyone raging at the screen, WINSTON looks around him, worried that he's been heard. But the Hate subsides as the THOUGHTCRIMINAL is seen again:

VOICE   What do you want to say to Big Brother now?

,

THOUGHTCRIMINAL I want to say…

The THOUGHTCRIMINAL *smiles, sincerely.*

Thank you. Thank you.

The THOUGHTCRIMINAL*'s head is pushed downward and a gun put to the back of it. He is shot. Blood spatters. Cheers from the crowd who then chant the slogans of Oceania. Some of them hold their hands in the air.*

We are left with the three slogans of the Party on the screen.

WAR IS PEACE

FREEDOM IS SLAVERY

IGNORANCE IS STRENGTH

A klaxon sounds.

TELESCREEN   Eleven hundred and two. Two Minutes
                    Hate is over, comrades.

JULIA *violently collides with someone, and is sent backwards, scattering chairs, she cries out in pain.* WINSTON *instinctively moves to help her then realises who it is. He is still terrified of her.*

WINSTON   You're hurt?

JULIA   It's nothing. It'll be all right in a second.

WINSTON   Nothing broken?

JULIA   Nothing broken. I'm all right. I'll be all
                    right in a moment.

JULIA *holds out her hand for him to help her. It seems like a trap.* WINSTON *helps her up.*

It's nothing. Really. Thank you.

She releases his hand and exists. WINSTON *is aware of something having been passed to him. As she shuts the door, he's alone.*

He opens his hand. Inside is a scrap of paper, folded.

He is terrified. He checks that he's alone and turns his back to the telescreen. He unfolds the message.

WINSTON   She's thoughtpolice. She knows. She's –

He now sees what is written – in large, uniformed handwriting: 'I love you'.

WINSTON is overcome.

A klaxon sounds. People pour into the canteen again. WINSTON 'comes to'. He knows he's been here before.

MARTIN   Victory gin!

SYME   You don't really appreciate Newspeak, Winston. Do you? Not really.

                        You don't have to be an expert to know that Newspeak is the only language in the world whose vocabulary gets smaller every year.

                        It's a beautiful thing, the destruction of words.

PARSONS   My kid made sure he was some kind of enemy agent. Might have been parachuted in or something. But this is the bit that's really brilliant. What put her onto him in the first place?

                                          ,

SYME   Shoes.

PARSONS   He was wearing a funny pair of shoes!

SYME   He told me before.

JULIA walks along the corridor as before. WINSTON watches her.

PARSONS   So chances are he was a foreigner. Pretty smart, right? Pretty smart for a seven year old.

JULIA enters the canteen.

                        Absolutely bursting with pride. You know what she did this weekend? Absolutely brilliant. Pleased as punch. Her troop are

on a patrol North West, heading towards
Willesden. And they hear something.
Whistling! Young man and woman from
the Ministry of Plenty, holding hands!
Stopped when they saw the kids of course.

But it was too late. That kind of behaviour.
Brazen.

SYME   Good.

PARSONS   I mean, there is a war on.

*JULIA comes closer, sits at the other end of the table. WINSTON, suddenly
reckless, nudges the tray off the table downstage towards her – everyone
else in the room stops as if there's been a gunshot.*

,

Be careful, comrade. Be careful.

JULIA moves in to help him clear it up. They're on the floor.

JULIA   Sunday afternoon?

WINSTON   Yes.

JULIA   At fifteen, get the train.

JULIA's voice seems to echo, and the canteen vanishes.

Get off at the third station. Turn left, follow
the path – wait at the biggest tree, the one
covered in moss. Wait for me.

*A sudden, two-second blackout – then a train whistle. The lights
come up. We are in the countryside.*

We're all right here.

WINSTON   We're all right here?

JULIA   Yes. We're miles from anywhere. Look at
the trees! Just don't go too far into the open.

,

I'm Julia.

39

'Hello Julia, I'm Winston Smith.'

WINSTON   How did you know that's –

JULIA   I'm careful. I'd be dead if I wasn't.

WINSTON   You've done this before?

JULIA   Hundreds of times. Well, a handful at least.

WINSTON   With Party members?

JULIA   Always.

WINSTON   The more men you've been with, the better.
                 I hate purity. I want the Party to rot from
                 the inside. To collapse in on itself. I want
                 corruption. Violence. Risk.

JULIA   You're going to love me.

                 ,

                 Oh – I've got a surprise.

She pulls out a slab of chocolate wrapped in silver paper.

WINSTON   Chocolate! I remember –

JULIA   It's real. Not like that crap the Party
                 rations out. This is the stuff they keep for
                 themselves.

WINSTON   How did you -

*She takes a small piece of chocolate and puts it into his mouth. They
stop still, her fingers lingering on his lips. He eats the chocolate, his
eyes closed. He opens them in joy at the taste. JULIA smiles.*

JULIA kisses him.

*They chase each other around the room, pulling things from the shelves,
throwing paper in the air and turning chairs over. Tiles drop from
the ceiling, panels fall from the walls. JULIA removes the red item of
clothing. They undress. They have sex as the sun deepens in colour.*

WINSTON   I feel like this has happened already. I
                 mean –

I've dreamt you.

I've dreamt this.

,

JULIA	How do you know you're not dreaming now?

,

WINSTON	Being with you the world feels solid. Real. I know who I am. I have memories. A past.
	The chocolate. It reminds me of – something.
	I can't remember.
JULIA	You thought I was an agent of the Thought Police.
WINSTON	Yes. I hated the sight of you. I wanted to murder you – I wanted to stab you in the throat. I wanted to smash your skull in.
JULIA	I'm a good liar. It's the only way to be safe.
WINSTON	Hardly safe to approach strangers -
JULIA	I detect the people who don't belong. There's something in your eyes that betrays you. I knew you were against them. I know everything about you.
WINSTON	You'd be useful to the Thought Police.

,

They'll kill us just for being here together. We'll end up in the Ministry of Love. It's inevitable.

JULIA	Nothing's inevitable.
WINSTON	Do you think they can be overthrown? That we can bring down the Party?

JULIA	We are.
WINSTON	I mean it.
JULIA	So do I. Being here. What we just did.
	It was a political act.
	,
	They want to abolish the orgasm. It's a threat to them. No love except love of Big Brother. No loyalty except to the Party. They keep everyone too miserable to notice what's going on. But once you see it – the Brotherhood, Goldstein, the war, it's all made up. Fictional. The hardest thing during the Two Minutes Hate is not to laugh.
WINSTON	But during the Hate you were screaming and shouting?
JULIA	What you say or do doesn't matter. Only feelings matter.
WINSTON	The Party is invincible. We can't defeat them. They always get you in the end. We're dead. We are the dead.
JULIA	We're not dead yet. This is ME. This is my hand.
	This is my neck. This is my head. And leg. And cheek. I'm alive. I'm REAL. I EXIST. Right now.
	We destroy the Party with tiny, secret acts of disobedience. Secret pleasures. It's possible to think something, to feel something that's just yours, that has nothing to do with them, even just for a second. Look.

She kisses him.

Simple as that. I just killed Big Brother.

,

WINSTON   Kill him again.

,

They look at each other.

JULIA   My train leaves in five minutes. Take the one after.

,

WINSTON   Oh.

JULIA   If you see me in the city don't stare. Don't smile. I won't acknowledge you. I can't protect you. This never happened.

WINSTON   This never happened.

JULIA   We may as well say goodbye.

WINSTON   Yes.

JULIA holds out her hand.

WINSTON shakes it but doesn't let go.

,

This is how it ends.

JULIA   We can't come here again. Not twice. It's too dangerous.

WINSTON   And to be together in the city... it's madness. We can't.

,

JULIA   We could...

WINSTON   It's suicide.

They stare into each other's eyes. A silence as they make a decision.

,

JULIA   We are the dead.

She moves to leave. Stops. Turns to him.

                           Find somewhere.

She exits.

We're back in the antique shop. CHARRINGTON moves to the cord and pulls it: the lights illuminate.

CHARRINGTON   The one place in the world where the past
                       still exists. My shop. Antiques. As was,
                       anyway: no-one wants old things any more.
                       There's another room in the back. Not even
                       a telescreen in there: never bothered.

WINSTON   No telescreen?

CHARRINGTON   It's just for storage, now, after all. There's a
                       little yard too. It's ragged, but it's discreet.
                       Used to be our garden.

                       Are you alright?

WINSTON   Yes. I've / been here before

CHARRINGTON   You've been here before. Bought the /
                       diary.

WINSTON   Keepsake album.

                           ,

CHARRINGTON   I'll rent it to you for very little. The room. If
                       you need somewhere. Everyone needs a bit
                       of privacy sometimes.

WINSTON looks around.

                           ,

WINSTON   Yes. Yes I'd like that. Thank you.

CHARRINGTON   Follow me then and we'll settle up. No
paperwork. No need to leave records.

CHARRINGTON gestures to the cupboard as before.

You'll do with a light.

It's just through there. Along the corridor.
It's the only door.

*WINSTON opens the cupboard door, which now opens onto a corridor.
He walks through the door. CHARRINGTON calls after him.*

Those pictures in there were wedding
presents. Couldn't bear to part with them.
And there's a bed. All antiques. Keep hold
of that key and you can come and go as it
suits you.

*WINSTON enters a small room full of beautiful antiques. Old furniture,
a threadbare carpet, peeling walls. A bed.*

WINSTON   Thank you.

He looks out of the window. He jumps on the bed.

No mics. No telescreen!

He looks up and sees JULIA, smiling.

JULIA   The size of the bed. For two people at once!

I've got a surprise. Here.

*She unloads a toolbox. Concealed in the base of it are various tins
and paper packets which she throws to WINSTON.*

Fresh bread. Jam. Milk. Real sugar!

WINSTON   How did you -

JULIA   Tea. There's been a lot of it about lately.
They've captured India or something.

He tickles her, she laughs and wriggles free.

And this is the one I'm most proud of!

She holds a package to WINSTON's face.

Real coffee from the Inner Party! TWO bags of –

She holds up a second bag, and coffee grains pour out.

They've chewed right through the paper! The city's swarming with rats. They're everywhere.

WINSTON   *(Quietly.)* Stop it.

JULIA   When hungry or agitated, rats can strip all the flesh from a human face in a matter of minutes. They show astonishing intelligence in knowing when someone is helpless.

WINSTON   *(Louder.)* Stop it stop it can you please stop it please please stop!

WINSTON is breathing heavily. He's trying not to vomit.

JULIA   What? Winston, what?

WINSTON   Anything but rats. Anything.

JULIA moves towards him and he flinches.

JULIA   Winston. You're shaking.

She puts her arms around him, cradling his head.

WINSTON   Anything. Anything but rats. Anything but rats. Please. Please. Anything.

JULIA   Look at me. They won't come in here. I'll plaster up every crack if necessary. We're alright here. We're alone. We're safe.

She sings to him, softly.

'Oranges and lemons', say the bells of St. Clement's.
'You owe me three farthings' say the bells of St Martins.
'When will you pay me?' say the bells of Old Bailey.

WINSTON   That song…

JULIA	I've seen oranges. They're a kind of fruit with a thick skin.
	I wonder what a lemon was.
WINSTON	How do you know that song?
JULIA	I've always known it.
WINSTON	But I didn't show you did I? The object, the – you weren't with me when -
JULIA	My grandfather sang it to me.
WINSTON	Your grandfather?
JULIA	Yes.
WINSTON	What else did / he - ?
JULIA	He was unpersoned when I was eight.
WINSTON	He must have told you things – about how things were before, before the Westminster bomb, before the Party took power.
JULIA	No.
WINSTON	There must be something.
JULIA	We should never have trusted them. We should never have trusted them. He said that over and over.
	I'm not the enemy, Winston.
WINSTON	This is all wrong. This is all wrong.
JULIA	Go outside.
WINSTON	What?
JULIA	Go outside. Into the yard.
	Trust me.

WINSTON leaves the room. For a moment, JULIA stays looking at the snowglobe, and then puts it down. The snow falls around the church.

WINSTON enters the yard. A helicopter passes overhead. He watches the MOTHER. She is singing.

MOTHER *(Singing)*   *They say that time heals all things,*
They say you can always forget,
But the smiles and the tears across the years
They twist my heart strings yet.

WINSTON   How does she do that?

How does she take a song written by a machine and give it…

I don't know.

Life.

JULIA appears in the doorway. WINSTON turns to JULIA and almost doesn't recognise her. She's wearing a red dress and her hair is down.

JULIA   *(Off.)* Turn around.

(Enters.) Here I can be a real woman, not a party comrade. We can be together here. In secret. This is the one place in the world where the past still exists. This is victory.

What's the matter?

WINSTON   I just… I wish there were words. There used to be words. For moments like this. For how I feel. For you. They're changing everything. Everything's *going*.

JULIA   Words don't matter.

WINSTON   Words matter. Facts matter. The *truth* matters. Look… every day I sit at a screen. I follow instructions. I correct articles – I mean, I delete things from records. Photographs.

People.

Like your grandfather.

JULIA   You delete –

WINSTON   Yes.

I delete people.

,

I could have done something.

Jones, Aaronson and Rutherford, three men accused of plotting major attacks, synchronised attacks in three locations around the globe on the Day of Plenty. They were caught and they confessed.

But years later, I was unwriting something in some edition of The Times, something unrelated, and I saw them. In a photograph. Jones, Aaronson and Rutherford, all three of them, smiling, in a café under a huge pink umbrella. And the photograph was dated the Day of Plenty. The day they were supposed to have been –

JULIA   So they weren't criminals?

WINSTON   They couldn't have been. In that one instance, one instance in my whole life, I possessed actual evidence *after* the event.

JULIA   What happened / to it?

WINSTON   I deleted it.

,

JULIA   Come back inside.

WINSTON   Now, this week, we're removing every scrap of evidence that we were ever at war with Eurasia or at peace with Eastasia.

JULIA   I thought we'd always been at war with Eastasia.

This frightens WINSTON. He breaks away from her.

WINSTON   What did you say?

JULIA shrugs.

JULIA	Who cares? It's all lies anyway. You just / said so.
WINSTON	How can you not remember that / we've –
JULIA	There's nothing we can do so why waste our time together talking about it?
WINSTON	But you're being *lied* to!
JULIA	I can't change anything so why should I let it / upset me?
WINSTON	How can you not want / to –
JULIA	If I engaged with it, if I really let myself think about it for any length of time I'd / go insane.
WINSTON	Don't you understand? History has *stopped.* Nothing *exists* except an endless present in which the Party is / always right.
JULIA	I don't *care* Winston. Honestly? It's boring.
WINSTON	We have to *do* something. Even if it's only for the next generation.
JULIA	I'm not interested in the next generation. I'm interested in *us.*
WINSTON	YOU'RE ONLY A REBEL FROM THE WAIST DOWNWARDS.

,

They are shocked into silence. Suddenly, JULIA explodes with laughter. WINSTON is confused, then relieved, then he laughs too. They laugh together, hard.

,

Nothing is ours. Nothing.

JULIA	Where are you now, Winston? This is ours. Our room. The present moment. *This is ours.*

,

WINSTON	It's not enough.

,

A slight divide between them. JULIA is hurt.

A klaxon sounds. The canteen reforms itself on stage, exactly as before – only, no SYME. His seat is conspicuously empty.

WINSTON looks around for SYME.

MARTIN	Victory gin!

PARSONS apparently talks to SYME'S empty chair.

PARSONS	My kid made sure he was some kind of enemy agent. Might have been parachuted in or something. But this is the bit that's really brilliant. What put her onto him in the first place?

,

He was wearing a funny pair of shoes! So chances are he was a foreigner. Pretty smart, right? Pretty smart for a seven year old.

WINSTON	Where's – ?

O'BRIEN is in the corridor.

PARSONS	I'm glad they watch us. I am. There are people out there who hate us. Hate our way of life. And if we're being watched, so are they.
WINSTON	What happened to – ?

PARSONS   Couldn't say. But wouldn't be surprised if
                 it's –

PARSONS aims an imaginary rifle and clicks his tongue.

                 ,

*O'BRIEN is still in the corridor – but amplified into the room, just as
he is when he and WINSTON talk.*

O'BRIEN   Winston. Winston Smith?

*A klaxon sounds. PARSONS checks his watch, collects his tray and
starts to leave.*

PARSONS   I mean, there is a war on.

O'BRIEN settles his glasses.

WINSTON   O'Brien?

O'BRIEN   I had been hoping for an opportunity of
                 talking to you. You take a scholarly interest
                 in Newspeak, I believe?

WINSTON   Hardly scholarly. I've never had anything
                 to do with the actual construction of the
                 language.

O'BRIEN   But you write it very elegantly. That is
                 not only my own opinion. I was talking
                 recently to a friend of yours who is
                 certainly an expert. His name has slipped
                 my memory for the moment.

WINSTON turns to look at SYME'S vacant chair.

A pause. They look at each other.

O'BRIEN resettles his spectacles on his nose.

                 I have an advanced copy of the tenth
                 edition of the Newspeak Dictionary. Some
                 of the new developments are ingenious. It
                 might interest you to look at it?

PARSONS checks his watch, collects his tray and starts to leave.

WINSTON   Very much. Yes. It would.

O'BRIEN   You could pick it up at my apartment. Let
           me give you my address.

*O'BRIEN writes in a notebook, tears the page out, folds it and gives
it to WINSTON.*

           I'm usually at home in the evenings. If not,
           my servant will give you the Dictionary.

*WINSTON comes back into the main room, holding a scrap of paper.
A memory of holding the scrap of paper from JULIA.*

*The antique shop room again. JULIA wakes up alone in the antique
shop room.*

JULIA   Winston? Winston?

WINSTON   I remember. I finally remember. The
           chocolate. My memory was completely
           wrong.

           My mother.

*The MOTHER becomes WINSTON'S MOTHER; the lights change; soundscape
shifts. WINSTON'S SISTER, the CHILD, sits somewhere on stage.*

           I was a boy. Ten or eleven. And I kept
           asking her – where's father?

MOTHER   You know the answer to that, Winston.
           You've always known it. I don't know why
           you want to torment me by asking it.

WINSTON   I was starving. My guts twisted.

MOTHER keeps on cleaning.

MOTHER   You can't be hungry, Winston. You've had
           more than your share already.

SISTER   Can I have some chocolate?

MOTHER   There isn't any chocolate.

A memory of earlier.

WINSTON	There is. I know there is.
MOTHER	Winston.
WINSTON	Did you pick up the ration today like you said?
MOTHER	I was going to save it, so we'd have something to look forward to.
WINSTON	I want it now. And I should have more than a third.
MOTHER	Don't be greedy.
WINSTON	I should. I'm young. I'm growing. I need to *eat*.
MOTHER	Winston
WINSTON	My stomach is clawing me.
MOTHER	Winston. You can have mine.
WINSTON	And hers.
MOTHER	Don't be so greedy. You're her big brother. She deserves some / too.
WINSTON	I WANT IT – I NEED IT.
MOTHER	Winston – I can't bear this. Right.

She takes out the chocolate.

	There are four squares. You can have three. You can have mine. And one for your sister.
WINSTON	I took all four – I snatched it from my sister's hand. I ran and hid and ate it all –
MOTHER	Winston!
WINSTON	Mother was calling out to me.
MOTHER	Winston!
WINSTON	And my sister crying.
JULIA	You were her big brother.

WINSTON	When I finally went home, all their things were there. But the house was empty. They'd vanished.
JULIA/MOTHER	Winston –
WINSTON	My mother wasn't extraordinary or anything, but she protected my sister –
JULIA	Winston –
WINSTON	– and she was prepared to sacrifice herself, to give everything up, for us. We were the future, she was the dead.
JULIA	Winston –
WINSTON	And now it's my turn.
	I should go. Now. To O'Brien.
	If anyone can change things, it's someone like him, someone with *power*. If O'Brien is what we think – and that conversation, if he meant what we think he meant, I'm going to go to him and declare myself an enemy of the Party. He was talking about Syme being –
JULIA	Unpersoned.

A chill.

WINSTON	I hate them. I hate the Party. I hate Big Brother. I hate the feelings that I feel because of them. I want to tear them down like - like clothes from a washing line.
JULIA	I think everybody / feels like that.
WINSTON	We're only the start of this. But if we act, then people will pick up where we leave off and it will build and build until the people take back the power. Those at the very bottom of the pile. If there's hope – real

	hope – it lies with them. In their future. We are / the
JULIA	The dead. I know. I know.
	I'm just…
	I'm frightened.
WINSTON	If I'm mistaken I'll look at the new Dictionary and then walk away.

JULIA wants to believe this is true.

> But I'm not mistaken. You know that.
>
> ,

JULIA	We'll have to travel separately.

WINSTON looks at her.

> It's madness but…
>
> I'm coming with you.
>
> Not for Goldstein or for O'Brien or the Brotherhood.
>
> For you.
>
> ,

WINSTON	I love you.

> ,

JULIA	Go.
	I'll meet you there.

O'BRIEN'S apartment. The telescreen chatters in the background. O'BRIEN consults a document and speaks into something in his hand.

O'BRIEN	Items one comma five comma seven approved fullwise stop suggestion contained item six doubleplus ridiculous verging crimethink cancel stop unproceed constructionwise antegetting plusfull

estimates machinery overheads stop end message.

Winston Smith.

O'BRIEN turns off the telescreen. The first real silence in the play.

WINSTON	You can switch it off!
O'BRIEN	We can switch it off. We have that privilege.
	Do you know where you are, Winston?
WINSTON	I think – the apartments of the Inner Party. I've never been here before.
O'BRIEN	Yes.
	,
	Well. Shall I say it or will you?
WINSTON	Is it – ?
O'BRIEN	Switched off. We are alone.
WINSTON	We believe that there is some kind of conspiracy, a secret organisation working against the Party and we want to join it. And work for it. We are enemies of the Party. We are thoughtcriminals. And we are at your mercy: if you want to incriminate us, well, then we are ready.

He takes JULIA's hand.

The door opens again – WINSTON and JULIA jump. MARTIN brings in a wine decanter and four glasses.

O'BRIEN	Come in. Take a seat.

There's a nervous pause as all four sit down – WINSTON notes MARTIN, who sits down.

Martin is one of us.

WINSTON and JULIA look at each other. O'BRIEN takes the decanter and glasses and pours.

It is called wine. You will have read about it, no doubt – you might even remember it? Not much of it gets to the Outer Party, I'm afraid. Our Leader –

He raises his glass – the others follow.

'

– Emmanuel Goldstein.

'

WINSTON is elated.

WINSTON	Then – then Goldstein is a real person.
O'BRIEN	Yes. Goldstein lives. Where, I don't know. But he's alive.
WINSTON	And the conspiracy, the organisation – it's real? Not just invented by the Thought Police?
O'BRIEN	The Brotherhood is real. You will never know much more about it than that it exists and that you belong to it. But we will come back to that.

Look. Time is against us. You shouldn't have come here together, and you must leave separately – you, Comrade *(JULIA.)* will leave first. You will understand, of course, that I have to begin by asking you certain questions. In general terms, what are you prepared to do? |
WINSTON	Anything.
O'BRIEN	You are prepared to sacrifice your lives?
WINSTON	Yes.
O'BRIEN	You are prepared to commit murder?
WINSTON	Yes.

O'BRIEN	To commit acts which may cause thousands of innocent deaths?
WINSTON	Yes.
O'BRIEN	You are prepared to lie, to forge, to blackmail, to recruit even the youngest children, to distribute drugs, to disseminate disease – to do anything which might weaken the power of the Party?
WINSTON	Yes.
O'BRIEN	To betray your country?
WINSTON	Yes.
O'BRIEN	If, for example, it would somehow serve our interests to throw sulphuric acid in a child's face – are you prepared to do that?
WINSTON	Yes.
O'BRIEN	You are prepared to commit suicide, if and when we order you to do so?
WINSTON	Yes.
O'BRIEN	You are prepared to lose your identity – forgo who you are – or to live in hiding?
WINSTON	Yes.
O'BRIEN	You are prepared never to see each other again?
JULIA	NO.
	,
WINSTON	No.
O'BRIEN	You did well to tell me. Comrade, even if he survives, it may be as a different person. We may be obliged to give him a new identity. His face, his age, his movements, the colour of his eyes, the shape of his

hands – his voice – could all be different. Our surgeons can alter people beyond recognition.

MARTIN moves, attracting WINSTON'S attention.

You will never know how many members the Brotherhood has: not even Goldstein himself, if he fell into the hands of the Thought Police, could give them a complete list. No such list exists. When you are caught, there will be hardly anyone you can betray. Ignorance is strength.

Understand that you will be fighting in the dark. You will always be in the dark. Orders will come and you will obey them and you will never know the specifics of why.

The Brotherhood does not exist in the ordinary sense – nothing holds it together, except an idea which is indestructible. An idea for, and a dream of, *the future.* That idea will sustain you.

There is no possibility that any perceptible change will happen within our lifetime. We are the dead. But our true life is in the future. I will send you the book in which this idea is expressed – Goldstein's book – which you will read and then destroy. Once you have finished the book, you will be full members of the Brotherhood – and you will then understand the true reality of things.

WINSTON   The true reality of things.

WINSTON can hardly believe it. He feels relaxed. O'BRIEN turns to JULIA.

O'BRIEN   You should leave us, Comrade. Martin, before you go – take a good look at these faces. You may be seeing them again.

MARTIN looks, expressionless, dispassionate, then fills the glasses again.

Well, Winston, what shall it be? To the
death of Big Brother? To humanity? To the
future?

WINSTON   To the past.

O'BRIEN and WINSTON look at each other in understanding.

O'BRIEN   The past is more important.

They drink to the past. O'BRIEN gives WINSTON and JULIA a white tablet.

Place it on your tongue. It will dissolve. It
is important for you not to leave smelling
of wine.

*MARTIN shows JULIA out, taking glasses and decanter. WINSTON and
O'BRIEN are alone. An odd, charged tension between them.*

Before you leave, do you have any
questions?

                       ,

WINSTON   Any question I like?

                       Is it –

O'BRIEN   Switched off.

                       ,

WINSTON   Did you ever hear an old rhyme that begins

                       '*Oranges and lemons', say the bells of St Clements,
                       'You owe me –*

WINSTON and O'BRIEN both say the next line – then O'BRIEN continues.

O'BRIEN   *– three farthings', say the bells of St Martin's.
                       'When will you pay me?' say the bells of Old Bailey.
                       'When I grow rich', say the bells of Shoreditch.*

WINSTON   You know it. You know how it ends.

O'BRIEN   I know how it ends.

                       ,

One thing left. The book.

To become a member of the Brotherhood you must read the book.

WINSTON   The book?

O'BRIEN   Goldstein's book. Once you finish it you will belong to the Brotherhood – and you will understand the true reality of things.

WINSTON   The true reality of things.

O'BRIEN   The copies are handwritten and there are not many in existence at any moment, but whenever I can get one, the following will happen.

The lights and sound are changing.

Winston – where do you think you are?

The sounds of a street. People enter.

WINSTON   I'm – I'm in a street. I think I'm in a street.

O'BRIEN   Good. Someone will touch you on the arm, and he will say –

MARTIN enters again, holding a briefcase. He grasps WINSTON's shoulder, presses the briefcase onto him, and exits.

O'BRIEN / MARTIN   I think you have dropped your briefcase.

WINSTON   Yes.

O'BRIEN   And in that briefcase will be Goldstein's book.

WINSTON opens the briefcase. Holds the book, and the street stops to look at him, encouraging. The people from the COMPANY at the beginning of the play. It feels almost like a ceremony. Lights flicker.

This book has been read in secret by hundreds of people like us who held in their hearts the same ideals and principles as we do. You will read it and then destroy the copy.

MARTIN	Once you finish this book you become a different person. You don't feel the same. You don't *think* the same. It changes everything. And it will always be true. It's a vision of the future no matter when it's being read.
O'BRIEN	Its readers are the Brotherhood, spread across the world, known only to themselves and not to each other. But we all read and rejoice in this book – and ensure that its light never goes out. We never forget that an idea is the only thing that has ever changed the world.

The COMPANY *applauds* WINSTON.

We shall meet again –

WINSTON	In the place where there is no darkness.
O'BRIEN	Yes.

Antiques shop room.

WINSTON	I've got *the book*.
JULIA	Oh. Good. Coffee?

WINSTON *takes the book from the case. It is the book from the start of the play. He reads.*

WINSTON   The Theory and Practice of Oligarchical Collectivism by Emmanuel Goldstein.

Chapter One. Ignorance is Strength.

WINSTON *closes the book. He is euphoric.*

I'm reading! There's no telescreen, no one watching or listening, I don't have to look over my shoulder or cover the page with my hand!

JULIA *gets ready for bed.*

Is this bliss?

,

I don't know where to start!

He opens the book at random.

Chapter Three. War is Peace.

The splitting-up of the world into three great superstates was an event which could be and indeed was foreseen before the middle of the twentieth century. In one combination or another, these three superstates are permanently at war. War hysteria is continuous and universal in all countries.

JULIA gets into bed. WINSTON continues to read, finding a section of particular interest.

Doublethink means the power of holding two contradictory beliefs in one's mind simultaneously, and accepting both of them. To tell deliberate lies while genuinely believing in them, to deny the existence of objective reality and all the while to take account of the reality which one denies – this is indispensably necessary.

He skips again to nearer the end.

Here we reach the central secret, the original motive, the never-questioned instinct that first led to the seizure of power and brought doublethink, the Thought Police, continuous warfare, and all the other necessary paraphernalia into existence afterwards.

He looks to JULIA. She is asleep.

This motive really consists…

He closes the book. WINSTON never reads of what this motive really consists. JULIA is asleep.

,

I'm not mad.

,

Being in a minority, even a minority of one, does not make you mad.

There is truth and there are lies. If you hold onto truth, even if the whole world is shouting against you, you're not mad.

Sanity is not statistical.

He gets into bed.

Sanity is not statistical.

He smiles. He likes the phrase.

He closes his eyes. The sun begins to rise. A low, rumbling sound, building and building until, suddenly, WINSTON wakes up with a start, screaming. JULIA stirs and places a hand on his face. WINSTON tries to catch his breath.

Where am I?

JULIA laughs, sleepily.

JULIA   Where do you think you are Winston?

,

WINSTON   I had a nightmare. The worst thing in the world.

JULIA puts an arm around him.

JULIA   You're safe. You're here.

She puts her arms around him as before. Outside, the MOTHER is singing.

MOTHER   *It was only a hopeless fancy,*
              It passed like an April day,
              But a look and a word and the dreams they stirred

–

They have stolen my heart away.

JULIA	Did you finish the book?
WINSTON	Yes. No. Nearly.

,

JULIA	So. What happens now?
WINSTON	We await our instructions.

,

JULIA	I will never betray you.
WINSTON	I will never betray you.
JULIA	Once they get us, we'll confess. Everybody always confesses. They'll torture us until we do.
WINSTON	Confession isn't betrayal. What you say to them doesn't matter. It's what you feel inside that matters.
JULIA	No matter what happens. There's something of me that can never be destroyed. And it belongs to you. It always will.

She holds his head in her hands.

In here.

,

I'm hungry. Let's have some coffee.

Real coffee. Is it late or is it early? The clock must have stopped.

WINSTON looks out of the window.

MOTHER	*They say that time heals all things,* *They say you can always forget;*

But the smiles and the tears across the years,
They twist my heart strings yet.

WINSTON   She's beautiful.

JULIA   She's a metre wide.

WINSTON   That's her style of beauty.

JULIA   She's had a hundred children.

We'll never have that.

WINSTON   What?

JULIA   Family.

,

WINSTON   All she does is work. All she's ever done.
And she's *singing.*

All over the world, millions, billions
of people just like her. Ignorant of one
another's existence, held apart by walls of
hatred and lies, and yet almost exactly the
same.

WINSTON feels a mystical reverence for the MOTHER.

People who have never learned to think
but who are storing up in their hearts and
minds and muscles the power that will one
day overturn the world. If there is hope it
lies in people like her. And her children,
and grandchildren and their children after
them.

In people. People are always just the same.
That's the message of Goldstein's book.

JULIA   You've not finished it.

WINSTON   I don't need to. Of course it is. The future is
theirs. A world of sanity.

JULIA   Sanity?

ORWELL / ICKE & MACMILLAN

WINSTON	Where there is equality there can be sanity. It's going to happen. Look at her.

The sun comes out from behind the cloud and slowly rises in intensity.

	All round the world, in London and New York, in Egypt and Beijing and in the furthest peasant village beyond the farthest frontier, in the streets of the cities, in the villages, the bazaars and the markets, everywhere, everywhere the eye can see, is the same solid, unconquerable woman –
JULIA	Winston –
WINSTON	A metre-wide from childbearing, working, toiling from birth to death –
JULIA	Winston –
WINSTON	Still singing.
JULIA	Winston.

The MOTHER's voice rises and all else is silent.

WINSTON	You were the dead; theirs was the future. But you could share in that future if you kept alive the mind as they kept alive the body, and passed on the secret doctrine that two plus two make four.
JULIA	Winston –
WINSTON	Julia.
JULIA	I love you.

,

He looks into her eyes. The MOTHER has ended her song. Everything is utterly silent.

WINSTON smiles.

WINSTON	We are the dead.

,

JULIA   We are the dead.

,

VOICE   YOU ARE THE DEAD.

WINSTON and JULIA spring apart. All blood rushes from their faces. The voice is metallic, unreal, terrifying. WINSTON and JULIA freeze.

               YOU ARE THE DEAD.

JULIA   They can see us.

VOICE   WE CAN SEE YOU.

               REMAIN EXACTLY WHERE YOU
               ARE. MAKE NO MOVEMENT UNTIL
               YOU ARE ORDERED.

WINSTON   It's starting. It's starting at last.

VOICE   IT'S STARTING.

JULIA   I suppose we may as well say goodbye.

VOICE   YOU MAY AS WELL SAY GOODBYE.

Suddenly there is an almighty crash and countless MEN IN UNIFORM flood into the room and set about dismantling it. It is terrifying and completely disorientating; the whole world changes.

A bag is put over JULIA'S head and she is taken swiftly from the room.

WINSTON   JULIA!

WINSTON is restrained.

Into the chaos walks CHARRINGTON, calmly. The MEN IN UNIFORM acknowledge his presence, becoming more subdued.

CHARRINGTON removes his glasses, then his white hair, revealing black hair beneath. He adjusts his posture, standing up straight. He is some twenty years younger than he has previously appeared.

CHARRINGTON   And by the way, while we're on the subject,
'here comes a candle to light you to bed,
here comes a chopper to chop off your head.'

A bag is put over WINSTON'S head. He is dressed in blue overalls by the guards.

Though nowhere to be seen, we hear O'BRIEN'S voice.

O'BRIEN *(Unseen.)*   Where do you think you are Winston?

WINSTON   Love.

O'BRIEN *(Unseen.)*   Where?

,

WINSTON   I think I'm

I think I'm in the Ministry of Love.

Another VOICE yells from the darkness, amplified by the mics.

VOICE   REMAIN STILL.

O'BRIEN *(Unseen.)*   And how long have you been here?

WINSTON   I…

I don't know.

Hours?

Days?

Weeks?

How long have I –

He is interrupted by a sudden scream of agony from a room nearby, creating a howl of feedback. It sounded like JULIA.

PARSONS emerges from the darkness. He also has a bag over his head and his hands tied. He has been beaten.

PARSONS   Winston? Winston is that you?

WINSTON turns towards the man.

VOICE   REMAIN STILL.

PARSONS   It's me. Parsons.

PARSONS shuffles towards WINSTON.

WINSTON   Parsons? What are you here for?

PARSONS   Thoughtcrime.

The word reverberates in the amplified room.

I never knew I had a bad thought in my head! I was sleeping! I was talking in my sleep! Shouting.

DOWN WITH BIG BROTHER!
DOWN WITH BIG BROTHER!
DOWN WITH BIG BROTHER!
DOWN WITH BIG BROTHER!
DOWN WITH BIG BROTHER!

Several MEN IN UNIFORM emerge from the darkness and stand nearby. They wear helmets which mask their faces.

WINSTON   How did they know?

PARSONS   How do you think?

My little girl! Listened through the keyhole. Went right to the patrols first thing in the morning. Pretty smart for a seven year old. I'm so proud of her. She'll be right at the front when they shoot me.

You know what I'm going to say right at the end? Last words?

'Thank you for saving me before it was too late.'

'Thank you.'

O'BRIEN *(Unseen.)*   Room 101.

The amplified voice becomes a piercing scream of feedback. PARSONS is suddenly terrified. The MEN IN UNIFORM restrain PARSONS and take him away. PARSONS struggles.

PARSONS   NO! PLEASE NO! ANYTHING BUT
THAT! I'LL DO ANYTHING! I'LL
CONFESS TO ANYTHING! SHOOT
ME! CUT MY THROAT! ANYTHING
BUT ROOM 101!

The words howl around the room. PARSONS has gone.

WINSTON   What's in Room 101?

*A WOMAN emerges from the darkness. She also has a bag over her head
and her hands tied.*

WOMAN   What's your name?

WINSTON is startled.

WINSTON   Smith.

WOMAN   That's funny. My name's Smith too. I might
be your mother.

Another scream from nearby.

           I had a son. He'd be about your age.

*WINSTON pulls the bag off the WOMAN'S head and touches her face. It
is JULIA. She looks completely different. She laughs. She jumps into
the arms of one of the MEN IN UNIFORM and they dance off together.*

The CHILD runs laps around the stage.

The MEN IN UNIFORM have surrounded WINSTON.

WINSTON   WHAT'S IN ROOM 101?

           WHAT'S IN ROOM 101?

O'BRIEN enters.

O'BRIEN   Now Winston, you know that already.
You've always known it.

WINSTON   O'Brien? They've got you too!

O'BRIEN   They got me a long time ago.

WINSTON   Where am I?

O'BRIEN   Where do you think you are Winston?

WINSTON reaches out towards one of the MEN IN UNIFORM and slowly pulls off the man's mask. The man has WINSTON'S face. The man with WINSTON'S face begins screaming.

Suddenly, WINSTON wakes up with a start, screaming. He is back in the room above the antique shop. He is panicked. He checks his surroundings. JULIA is next to him. She stirs and places a hand on his face. WINSTON tries to catch his breath.

WINSTON   Where am I?

JULIA laughs, sleepily.

JULIA   Where do you think you are Winston?

,

WINSTON   I had a nightmare. The worst thing in the world.

JULIA puts an arm around him.

JULIA   Room 101.

                    You know what's in Room 101, Winston.

WINSTON turns to her. She speaks in O'BRIEN'S voice.

                    You've always known it.

WINSTON   What did you say?

JULIA   I.

                    Love.

WINSTON   Julia? What's – ?

JULIA   The Ministry of Love.

,

                    And that's where you are now.

                    Look.

WINSTON 'comes to'.

O'BRIEN   I told you that if we met again it would be in the place where there is no darkness.

WINSTON   Yes.

Lights flicker on. Bright, uncomfortable, unforgiving, but illogical, the room is somehow endless.

O'BRIEN   You know why you are here. You know what has to happen. You've known for a long time.

You suffer from a defective memory. You are unable to remember real events and you persuade yourself that you remember other events which never happened.

O'BRIEN settles his glasses.

But this is curable. And once you are cured, you will feel better than you have ever felt. No false memories. You will love Big Brother. You'll be *happy*. Right now, you are a minority of one. You have chosen to be a madman.

WINSTON   Sanity is not statistical.

The words 'Sanity is not statistical' appear all around.

O'BRIEN   I know your mind Winston. I know what you've been thinking. What you're thinking now and what you're yet to think. I've watched you for longer than you can imagine.

Trust me, Winston. I'm going to make you perfect. It's time.

Several TORTURERS enter the room. WINSTON watches them, fearfully.

Take a seat.

'

WINSTON sits, cautiously. The TORTURERS sit.

With which power is Oceania at war, at this moment?

'

Winston?

O'BRIEN'S manner is that of a doctor, a teacher, even a priest, anxious to explain and persuade.

WINSTON   When I was arrested, Oceania was at war with Eastasia.

O'BRIEN   With Eastasia. Good. And for how long has Oceania been at war with Eastasia?

WINSTON studies O'BRIEN'S face.

You're afraid to answer because you know that throughout this conversation, pain can be applied to you at any moment and to any degree.

But that pain will help you. Pain compels truth. And it is important you answer truthfully. Your truth, at least. Tell me what you think you remember.

,

WINSTON   Until recently we were not at war with Eastasia at all. We were their allies. The war was against Eurasia. That lasted for four years. And before that –

O'BRIEN signals to someone.

O'BRIEN   The fingertips.

Several TORTURERS stand, collect equipment from a trolley and move towards WINSTON. As the scalpel reaches his finger, a blackout.

The lights flicker on. WINSTON is red with pain, panting, and his fingertips have been removed. There's blood.

Another example. Jones, Aaronson and Rutherford, three men guilty of committing atrocities in three cities on the Day of Plenty. You believe that you saw proof of their innocence. A photograph.

WINSTON	Yes.

O'BRIEN produces a photograph.

O'BRIEN	This photograph.
WINSTON	YES! YES! That exact one! It exists! It EXISTS!
O'BRIEN	No, it does not exist.
WINSTON	It does! It's right there!
O'BRIEN	It does not exist. It never existed.

He destroys the photograph.

WINSTON	But it did – it does – exist. In memory. I remember it. It was there, a second ago – and we saw it. I remember it now. You remember it.
O'BRIEN	I do not remember it.
WINSTON	But –
O'BRIEN	I'm trying to help you Winston. To see the truth.

TORTURERS stand, move to the trolley and select pliers, a small metal drill, a cloth and a porcelain bowl.

WINSTON	But that's not the truth, the truth is…

The TORTURERS move towards WINSTON.

O'BRIEN	Does the past have real existence?

WINSTON squirms in the chair as the TORTURERS near him.

	Winston. Does the past have real existence?
	Is there a place in the world where the past still exists?
WINSTON	Antique shop. The one place in the world the past still exists.
O'BRIEN	Teeth.

A TORTURER pulls WINSTON's head back and we go to blackout.

As the lights come up, WINSTON vomits blood.

TORTURERS are strapping down WINSTON's arms.

O'BRIEN puts his hand on WINSTON's head, gently.

	You are afraid that something will break. Your particular fear is that it will be your backbone. You have a vivid mental picture of the vertebrae snapping apart and the spinal fluid dripping out of them. That is what you are thinking. No?
	I am taking time with you, Winston, because you are worth time.
	What year is it?
WINSTON	Nineteen…
	Two-thousand and…
O'BRIEN	Where does the past exist?
WINSTON	In records. Written down.
O'BRIEN	Where else?
WINSTON	In the mind. In human memory.
O'BRIEN	In records and human memory. Good. We, the Party, control all records and we control all memories. Then we control the past, do we not?

WINSTON is fighting back with everything he has.

WINSTON	But you can't stop people from remembering things! You can't control memory! You haven't controlled mine!

O'BRIEN remains unfazed.

O'BRIEN	No, Winston. *You* have not controlled yours. That's why you are here. You believe that reality is objective, external. That

reality exists in its own right. You think that if you can see it, then everyone else must see the same thing as you. But you are wrong. Reality exists only in the mind, and nowhere else. Not in the mind of the individual – which makes errors and will eventually die – but in the mind of the Party, which is accurate, collective and immortal.

The TORTURERS move to their equipment.

Power is power over people, Winston, yes, over the body, but above all, over the mind. Power over external, objective reality is not important.

The TORTURERS are attaching brightly coloured wires to WINSTON. A sponge is submerged in water then placed beneath a metal plate on WINSTON'S head.

Reality is inside the skull.

Do you remember writing that 'freedom is the freedom to say that two plus two make four'?

WINSTON   Yes.

O'BRIEN holds up four fingers.

O'BRIEN   How many fingers Winston?

WINSTON   Four.

O'BRIEN   And if the Party says that it is not four – but five. Then how many?

WINSTON   Four.

A massive surge of pain rushes through WINSTON. O'BRIEN'S fingers remain held up.

O'BRIEN   How many fingers, Winston?

WINSTON   Four.

Again, more pain.

O'BRIEN   How many fingers, Winston?

WINSTON   Four! Four! What else can I say! Four!

And more pain. WINSTON'S *head thrashes back and forwards.*

O'BRIEN   How many fingers, Winston?

WINSTON   FIVE! FIVE! FIVE!

,

O'BRIEN   No, Winston, that is no use. You are lying.
           You still think there are four. How many
           fingers, please?

WINSTON   Four! FIVE! FOUR! ANYTHING! STOP
           THE PAIN! STOP THE PAIN!

O'BRIEN   You are a slow learner, Winston.

WINSTON, *like a child, shivering, pleading, wanting approval.*

WINSTON   How can I help it? How can I help seeing
           what is in front of my eyes? Two and two
           are four.

O'BRIEN   Sometimes. Sometimes they are five.
           Sometimes they are three. Sometimes they
           are all of them at once.

           You must try harder – it is not easy to
           become sane.

           How many fingers Winston?

WINSTON   I don't know, I don't know, you will kill me
           if you do that again. Four, five, six, I don't
           know – in all honesty I don't know.

,

O'BRIEN   Better.

O'BRIEN *nods to one of the* TORTURERS, *who gives* WINSTON *some water
through a straw.*

You will give in eventually. The price of sanity is submission. Winston, we are curing you. We convert the heretic so that he is a heretic no longer: we make him one with us. We do not tolerate rebellion, even if it exists only in a brain awaiting a bullet. We make the brain perfect before we blow it out.

But you are not perfect yet. You still think you are the hero. You still believe that you are going to win. You picture the future. You have thought about it and thought about it.

WINSTON	Yes.
O'BRIEN	You were writing for them. The unborn.
WINSTON	Yes.
O'BRIEN	You hoped to inspire them to change things.
WINSTON	Yes!
O'BRIEN	You wanted to give them your message.
WINSTON	Yes!
O'BRIEN	Then go ahead. Speak to us.

A sudden, bright light on WINSTON. The house lights slowly rise.

WINSTON	I'm –
O'BRIEN	We're listening Winston. We're all watching you.

Silence. WINSTON is aware of us watching him.

What does the future look like? Tell us what will defeat the Party?

,

Go ahead. Winston, speak to us.

'

Winston? What will defeat us?

WINSTON	Brotherhood. Humanity. The spirit of Man.
O'BRIEN	Brotherhood. Humanity. The spirit of Man.
	And do you consider yourself a man?
WINSTON	Yes.
O'BRIEN	If you want a picture of the future, Winston, imagine a boot stamping on a human face – for ever. The face of the enemy. Defeated. Powerless. But about to be cured.
	If you want a picture of the future, the enemy of society will always be there, Goldstein will always be there, defeated and humiliated again and again and again.
	This drama that we have played out will be played out over and over again, generation after generation, victory after victory.
	This is the future. Right now.
	You have no past, Winston. You are deleted from history. If you are a man, Winston, you are the last man. No past. No future. Right now. But you still consider yourself morally superior to us?
	Winston?
WINSTON	Yes. Yes. I consider myself morally superior.

Footage plays from an earlier scene:

O'BRIEN	*You are prepared to commit murder?*
WINSTON	*Yes.*
O'BRIEN	*To commit acts which may cause thousands of innocent deaths?*
WINSTON	*Yes.*

O'BRIEN	*If, for example, it would somehow serve our interests to throw sulphuric acid in a child's face – are you prepared to dothat?*
WINSTON	*Yes.*

The footage ends.

O'BRIEN   Brotherhood. Humanity. The spirit of Man.

You wanted to speak. Tell us how the Party will fall. What will defeat us?

,

WINSTON   Love. Love.

,

O'BRIEN   Love is what will win? Your love for Julia, and her love for you, will bring everything crashing down?

WINSTON   Yes.

O'BRIEN   How?

How will that happen?

How can the love of two people, however strong, destroy the system which organises the entire world?

,

WINSTON   … I don't know.

O'BRIEN   Your love is the most important thing to *you* and to you alone. To the world, your love is meaningless. It achieves nothing, it serves no purpose. It makes no difference. The fact that you will never see Julia again does not change the world one iota.

It only matters to you. All you care about is yourself.

Even Big Brother, you thought, was watching you in particular. But Winston, your world consisted entirely of your own solipsism. Big Brother *is* you, watching.

If we consider your mind, your memories, your fears and your fantasies and your longing to be important, to be a hero, whether by writing a diary for a distant future or by changing the world as a member of the Brotherhood – if we consider all of these things, Winston – not one of them is about anything more or less than Winston Smith – and his vain, selfish, unimportant desires. Coffee. Chocolate. Sex. Love.

O'BRIEN holds WINSTON's head in his hands.

You're trapped in the centre of your self. Imprisoned in your own skull.

And we need to let you out, Winston, break you open and let you out into reality, beyond selfish obsessions and false memories, reality as the rest of us see it. The reality of the Party.

There is nothing that I could not do, Winston.

I could float six feet off the floor if I wanted to.

I could fly.

If that is the reality inside the mind of the Party.

The house lights fade. The TORTURERS stand, detach WINSTON from any equipment, organise the objects on the table and prepare to leave.

If you have any questions, you may ask them.

,

WINSTON   Any question I like?

The TORTURERS *have gone.* WINSTON *is safe from pain.*

WINSTON   Is it –

O'BRIEN   Switched off.

MARTIN *appears and hands a glass of wine to* O'BRIEN.

WINSTON   What have you done with Julia?

O'BRIEN   She betrayed you. Unreservedly. I have seldom seen anyone come over to us so promptly.

WINSTON   You tortured her?

,

Does Big Brother exist?

O'BRIEN   Of course he exists. The Party exists. Big Brother is the embodiment of the Party.

WINSTON   I mean – does he exist in the way I exist?

,

O'BRIEN   You do not exist.

WINSTON *struggles with this.*

WINSTON   I…

O'BRIEN   You do not exist Winston.

WINSTON   I think I exist. I was born. I'll die. I occupy space. Nothing else can occupy the same point simultaneously. In that sense – concretely – does Big Brother exist?

O'BRIEN	It is of no importance in what sense. He exists.
WINSTON	Will Big Brother ever die?
O'BRIEN	Of course not. How could he die?
WINSTON	Does the Brotherhood exist?
	,
O'BRIEN	Winston, if we set you free when we have finished here, and you live to be ninety years old, you will never learn the answer to that question. As long as you live, it will be an unsolved riddle in your mind.
	,
WINSTON	But the book – the book that –
O'BRIEN	I wrote it, Winston. That is, I collaborated in writing it.

MARTIN and O'BRIEN look at one another. MARTIN leaves.

WINSTON	Is it real – is it true – what it says?
O'BRIEN	As description, yes. The programme it sets forth is nonsense. The people are not going to revolt. They will not look up from their screens long enough to notice what's really happening.
	The individual is dead, Winston. The Party is immortal.

WINSTON is a wreck, barely alive.

And the Party will always win.

We are so nearly there. You are almost perfect. There is no pain you can now withstand. There is nothing to which you have not confessed. There is nothing left for you to hold on to.

WINSTON is barely able to speak.

WINSTON	One thing left.
O'BRIEN	I didn't hear you, Winston.

,

WINSTON looks at O'BRIEN. He is defiant.

WINSTON	One thing left.
	I never betrayed Julia.
	I never betrayed her.
O'BRIEN	No – no, that is perfectly true. You have not betrayed Julia.

,

When I told you that you could ask me anything, there was one question that immediately came to mind. You were afraid to ask it because you already knew the answer.

The worst thing in the world varies from individual to individual. It may be burial alive, or death by fire, or by drowning, or by impalement.

Ask the question Winston.

WINSTON	Where am I now?
O'BRIEN	Where do you think you are?
WINSTON	I think…
	I think this is Room 101.

,

O'BRIEN	And what's in Room 101?
WINSTON	The thing that's in Room 101 is the worst thing in the world.

An ANIMAL HANDLER wheels a trolley onto the stage with great care, accompanied by some TORTURERS. They wear thick gloves and protective masks. On the trolley is a large metal box.

O'BRIEN   In your case, Winston, the worst thing in the world happens to be rats.

WINSTON   No.

O'BRIEN   You understand this construction. The mask will fit over your head, leaving no exit. The rats will begin in the front section of the cage, with two gates between them and your face. Once the mask is installed the first gate will open and the rats, desperate to escape, will come closer. You will be able to smell them. You can bring things to a close whenever you choose. You know that. Nothing is happening that you did not foresee.

WINSTON   No. I can't. I can't.

O'BRIEN   The rats are starving. Once the second gate is opened, they will leap onto your face and bore straight into it. Sometimes they attack the eyes first. Sometimes the tongue.

We hear the rats – squealing, tearing, scratching.

WINSTON   Please. You can't.

O'BRIEN   It is an instinct which cannot be disobeyed. It is the same with you. They are a form of pressure that you cannot withstand, even if you wished to. You know what you need to do.

WINSTON   I don't! What is it? What is it? How can I do it if I don't know what –

O'BRIEN   Now, Winston, you know that already. You have always known it.

The word 'JULIA' appears.

The TORTURERS raise the contraption and prepare to attach it to WINSTON's face. WINSTON moans in terror.

> When hungry or agitated, rats can strip all the flesh from a human face in a matter of minutes.
>
> They show astonishing intelligence in knowing when someone is helpless.

WINSTON looks at people in the audience and pleads with them.

WINSTON   HOW CAN YOU JUST SIT THERE? GET UP! DO SOMETHING! HELP ME – HELP ME – YOU HAVE TO STOP THEM – PLEASE GET UP – PLEASE – I'M SORRY – NO – I'M SORRY

The mask is attached to WINSTON's face.

O'BRIEN   I am going to open the first gate.

WINSTON   STOP IT! PLEASE STOP – I CAN'T –

O'BRIEN opens the first gate.

O'BRIEN   I am your friend Winston. I'm trying to help you.

                 I am now going to open the second gate.

O'BRIEN prepares to open the gate.

Winston   JULIA! JULIA!

                 DO IT TO JULIA! DO IT TO JULIA! I DON'T CARE WHAT YOU DO TO HER. TEAR HER FACE OFF, RIP HER FLESH TO PIECES JUST DO IT TO HER! NOT ME! JULIA! JULIA! DO IT TO JULIA!

The lights black out. The sound of the rats is overwhelming.

Lights snap up.

WINSTON blinks and looks around. He no longer wears the mask.

He's sitting in a café. Music is playing, it's sunny. He sits under a pink umbrella and has a coffee cup in front of him.

The WAITRESS from the beginning of the play approaches. She pours coffee into the cup in front of WINSTON.

I betrayed you.

WAITRESS   Sorry?

WINSTON   I betrayed you.

She's a little confused.

WAITRESS   I betrayed you.

She gives him her full attention. She continues to pour the coffee. WINSTON mumbles along with her occasionally.

Sometimes they threaten you with something. Something you can't stand up to. Can't even think about. And then you say 'don't do it to me, do it to somebody else. Do it to…'

,

And perhaps you pretend, afterwards, that it was only a trick and you just said it to make them stop and didn't really mean it. But that isn't true. You think there's no other way of saving yourself, and you're quite ready to save yourself that way. You *want* it to happen to the other person.

As you betray them, in that moment, it's real. Whatever you say after. All you care about is yourself

WINSTON   All you care about is yourself.

WAITRESS   That moment is everything.

And afterwards, you don't feel the same towards the other person any more.

WINSTON   No. You don't feel the same…

The WAITRESS stops pouring the coffee.

,

WAITRESS   I was just asking if you were feeling unwell.

WINSTON 'comes to'.

WINSTON   Sorry. I was just… I was just… nothing.

                 False memory.

We hear a VOICE, as at the beginning of the play:

VOICE   He was troubled by false memories
                 occasionally, but they did not matter, so
                 long as one knew them for what they were.
                 Some things had happened, others had not
                 happened.

*MARTIN enters, reading from the book. He is followed by the COMPANY
from the beginning of the play. PARSONS is holding the CHILD's hand.
She runs and steals the chocolate from the saucer on WINSTON's table.*

MARTIN   But it was all right, everything was all right,
                 the struggle was finished. He had won the
                 victory over himself.

MOTHER   This is how it ends?

HOST   This is how it ends.

FATHER   Did this really happen?

                 I mean, were things really like this in
                 nineteen eighty-four or…

                 Because that was over a hundred years ago.

                 ,

                 This is a stupid question.

HOST   No – no, so far as we know, it happened. At
                 some point prior to 2050, the Party fell: we
                 know that. Well, here we are. And listen to

how we're speaking: no Newspeak. Though whether this account was actually written in 1984 as the first page claims – well, I wish I knew. There's just no evidence. Very little is known for certain.

We do know that Winston Smith himself never existed – outside the book, anyway. He's imagined.

WINSTON looks up, trying to comprehend this.

FATHER   So who wrote it?

HOST   Nobody knows. Over time, various authors have been suggested as the writer but none of them have ever been verified by birth records – or burial records. Could have been written collaboratively. Most likely, its real author was unpersoned.

              Of course, it's the text itself, the idea that's important – not the name written on the front of it.

FATHER   But Winston was imaginary?

HOST   He never existed. Though here we are. Still talking about him.

The book is placed on WINSTON's table.

WINSTON picks the book up.

CHILD   *'Oranges and lemons', say the bells of St Clement's,*
              'You owe me three farthings', say the bells of St Martin's,
              'When will you pay me?' say the bells of Old Bailey,
              'When I grow rich', say the bells of Shoreditch.
              'Pray when will that be?' say the bells of Stepney.
              'I do not know…'

MOTHER   But, I mean, wouldn't they…

              If the Party…

How do we know the Party fell? Wouldn't it be in their interest to just structure the world in such a way that we believed that they were no longer…

She loses her train of thought, shakes her head.

CHILD *Here comes a candle to light you to bed,*
Here comes a chopper to chop off your head.
Chop chop chop chop
The last man's dead.

MOTHER takes her daughter by the hand. They exit. The stage is now almost empty.

WINSTON becomes aware of O'BRIEN, watching him. WINSTON smiles at him, genuinely.

Silence.

,

WINSTON Thank you.

,

Blackout.

Headlong

Headlong: /hedl'ong/ noun 1. with head first, 2. starting boldly, 3. to approach with speed and vigour

Headlong creates exhilarating contemporary theatre – a provocative mix of innovative new writing, reimagined classics and influential twentieth century plays that illuminate our world.

Touring exceptional theatre around the UK lies at the heart of what we do; we also present work on major London stages and internationally.

We encourage the best emerging artists and more established talent to do their most exciting work with us. And we place digital innovation at the forefront of all our activities – building inventive online content to sit alongside our productions to enrich audiences' understanding of our work.

'A touring company of generous unpredictability'
The Observer

'The indefatigably inventive Headlong'
The Times

Artistic Director **Jeremy Herrin**
Executive Producer **Henny Finch**
Finance Manager **Julie Renwick**
Assistant Producer **Stephen Daly**
Administrative Assistant **Debbie Farquhar**
Creative Associate **Sam Potter**
Literary Associate **Duncan Macmillan**
Associate Artist **Sarah Grochala**
Marketing Consultant **Kym Bartlett**
Press Agent **Clióna Roberts**

www.headlong.co.uk
@HeadlongTheatre

David Beames and Stanley Townsend in *The Nether*
Photo: Johan Persson

Nottingham Playhouse

About Nottingham Playhouse Co-producer of 1984

Nottingham Playhouse first worked with Headlong in 2012, when we co-produced Robert Icke's imaginative reworking of **Romeo & Juliet**. We are delighted to be collaborating again to bring George Orwell's timeless classic **1984** to the stage.

Nottingham Playhouse has been one of the United Kingdom's leading producing theatres since our foundation in 1948. We welcome over 110,000 customers through our doors each year and create productions large and small: timeless classics, enthralling family shows and adventurous new commissions, often touring work nationally and internationally.

2013 marked our 50th anniversary in our current home. During those 50 years the Playhouse stage has played host to many outstanding performers and helped create a generation of dedicated theatre goers. Recent notable productions include **The Kite Runner**, Steven Berkoff's **Oedipus** and Brecht and Weill's **The Threepenny Opera**.

To find out more about our work please see **nottinghamplayhouse.co.uk** or call **0115 941 9419**.

 nottinghamplayhouse
 @NottmPlayhouse

Artistic Director Giles Croft
Chief Executive Stephanie Sirr

Nottingham Playhouse with Anish Kapoor's Sky Mirror outside
Photo: David Baird

Nottingham Playhouse is a registered charity no 1109342

ALMEIDA
THEATRE

A small room with an international reputation, the Almeida began life as a literary and scientific society – complete with library, lecture theatre and laboratory. From the very beginning, our building existed to investigate the world.

Today, we make bold new work that asks big questions: of plays, of theatre and how we live.

We bring together the most exciting artists to take risks; to provoke, inspire and surprise our audiences; to interrogate the present, dig up the past and imagine the future.

Whether new work or reinvigorated classic, whether in our theatre, on the road or online, the Almeida makes work to excite and entertain with extraordinary live art, every day.

Artistic Director **Rupert Goold**

Artistic Associate **Jenny Worton**

Associate Director **Robert Icke**

Oliver Chris and Tim Pigott-Smith in *King Charles III*
Photo: Johan Persson

Almeida Theatre, Almeida Street, London N1 1TA
Registered charity no. 282167

Discover almeida.co.uk | 020 7359 4404

Like /almeidatheatre
Follow @AlmeidaTheatre

Principal Partner

A S P E N

Supported using public funding by
ARTS COUNCIL
ENGLAND

WWW.OBERONBOOKS.COM

 Follow us on www.twitter.com/@oberonbooks
& www.facebook.com/OberonBooksLondon